Où est mon Ballon - Where is my ball?

A Bilingual Picture Story Book in English and French

for Young Children

Written by **Frederic Bibard**

Illustrated by **Fung Ming Wong**

Voice: **Frederic Bibard, Virginie Glardon / Brittany Lee, Sam Dhoss**

A Foreword For Parents

Dear Parents,
Thank you for choosing this bilingual story book. Raising your child to speak both French and English is not an easy task, so kudos to you
for taking it on This book should be a fun way to help you with that.
What you can expect from this book:

- A story that is especially created for very young children ages 0 – 6. It features carefully selected vocabulary to help kids learnbasic words like shapes, sizes, and colors, as well as how to introduce themselves.
- 30 different visual scenes created to stimulate the minds of young learners.
- The stories are written in parallel text, meaning each paragraph is written in both French and English.
- The book comes with a free audio. There are two audio files available: one in English with the story characters narrated by native English speakers, and another audio file in French with the characters narrated by French native speakers.

The audio is designed to be a perfect supplement to help young ones learn the correct pronunciation and improve their listening
skills as well. Plus, you can enjoy listening with your child, too!
Now that I have shared with you the features of this storybook, I won't keep you any longer — go ahead and enjoy this book
with your little one.

Have fun!
Frédéric BIBARD
Founder, Talk in French.com

Important ! To download the audio. Please go to the last page of this book

Mon ballon... Où est mon ballon ?
My ball... Where is my ball ?

Bonjour !
Hello!

5

Salut
Hi

Qui es tu ?
Who are you ?

Je suis un garçon
I am a boy

8

Comment tu t'appelles ?
What is your name ?

Je m'appelle Pierre. Et toi ?
My name is Pierre. And you ?

Je suis Marguerite
I am Daisy

Tu as quel âge ?
How old are you?

J'ai quatre ans
I am four years old

Moi j'ai... un, deux, trois, quatre, cinq ans
Me, I am... one, two, three, four, five years old

14

C'est mon ballon ?
It's my ball ?

15

Non, c'est mon ours en peluche
No, it's my teddy bear.

Je cherche mon ballon
I am looking for my ball

Il est petit ?
Is it small ?

18

Non, il est grand
No, it is big

Il est jaune
Is it yellow ?

Non, il est rouge
No, it is red

Oh, je vois ton ballon !
Oh, I see your ball !

Où ? Où ?
Where?Where ?

Ici !
Here !

Ce n'est pas mon ballon, c'est un chien !
It's not my ball, it's a dog !

Oui, c'est mon chien
Yes, it's my dog

Et mon ballon ?
And my ball ?

27

Il est là !
It is there !

28

Mon ballon !
My ball !

C'est ta maison ?
It's your house ?

30

Oui
Yes

Tu es ma voisine !
You are my neighbor!

Et tu es mon voisin !
And you are my neighbor !

A bientôt.
See you later !

Au revoir !
Good bye!

Conclusion

How was the story? Did you enjoy it? I hope you had a fun time finding the red ball. I would love to hear how you and your child enjoyed the story (or what parts you thought could use some work). Please send your feedback to contact@talkinfrench.com

You can also leave a review on Amazon. That would be greatly appreciated as well. If you need more materials related to learning

French, you can always visit my website, www.talkinfrench.com. It has plenty of articles that will help you teach yourself – and your child – to speak French. You can also find some helpful information about travelling in France.

Once again, thank you so much for buying this book.

Merci beaucoup.
Frédéric Bibard

How to download the audio

Please go to this page :

talkinfrench.com/children-story-ball

Trouble to download?

Contact me at contact@talkinfrench.com